LOVE, CRIME AND
JOHANNESBURG

'*I love my Bibi and I love my Lulu …*'
BABY CELE (Bibi Khuswayo), LINDANI NKOSI (Jimmy 'Long Legs'
Mangane) and GINA SHMUKLER (Lulu Levine)

LOVE, CRIME AND
JOHANNESBURG

Junction Avenue Theatre Company

WITWATERSRAND UNIVERSITY PRESS

Love, Crime and Johannesburg

© Junction Avenue Theatre Company

First published 2000

Reprinted 2005, 2006, 2011

Witwatersrand University Press
1 Jan Smuts Avenue
2001 Johannesburg
South Africa

Applications to perform this work in public and to obtain a
copy of the score should be made to:
Dramatic and Literary Rights Organisation (DALRO)
P O Box 31609
2017 Braamfontein

Typeset by Sue Sandrock
Photographs by Ruphin Coudyzer

ISBN-10: 1 86814 354 6
ISBN-13: 978 1 86814 354 2

Printed by Creda Communications

Love, Crime and Johannesburg was created in workshops by Malcolm Purkey and Carol Steinberg (writers) with: Xoli Norman, Ramolao Makhene, Arthur Molepo, Lawrence Joffe, Gina Shmukler, Tumisho Masha, Mmabatho Mogomotsi, Salvee Viljoen and Baby Cele.

It premièred at the Standard Bank National Arts Festival in July 1999 and was subsequently performed at the Market Theatre Johannesburg from 15 July to 4 September 1999 with Lindani Nkosi as Jimmy 'Long Legs' Mangane, Ramolao Makhene as Bones Shibambo, Arthur Molepo as Lewis Matome, Gina Shmukler as Lulu Levine, Baby Cele as Bibi Khuswayo, Linda Sebezo as Queenie Dlamini and Lawrence Joffe as Bokkie Levine.

Principal composition was by Ed Jordan and Arrangements and Musical Direction by Saranti Reeders. Additional composition was by Arthur Molepo, André Strijdom, Xoli Norman and Saranti Reeders. The production was designed by Sarah Roberts. The Lighting Designer was Declan Randall and the production was choreographed by Lindani Nkosi.

'Own the banks ...'
ARTHUR MOLEPO (Lewis Matome, Chairman of the Bank)

INTRODUCTION

———— • ————

'I know you'll think I'm mad, but I love Johannesburg'

In 1997, when Mzwakhe Mbuli, the people's poet, was arrested and accused of robbing a bank, we were truly amazed. Mbuli was an icon of the struggle, a hero of the young lions. He was a large, imposing figure of a man, his booming voice spoke to a generation. In the 1980s, during the most bitter years of struggle, he would perform his poetry at mass rallies and funerals in front of tens of thousands of people. He had a power and hypnotic authority that everybody knew was quite remarkable, even if many were unsure of the ultimate value of his poetry. How was it that such a shining figure could find himself in such a perverse mess?

Our amazement was compounded when Robert McBride, a most controversial soldier of the struggle, a death row prisoner, and then a Member of Parliament in South Africa's first democratic government, was arrested, accused of gunrunning and held in a Mozambican jail for six months without trial. How was this possible? What was going on? Had Robert McBride joined the ranks of the criminals, running guns into KwaZulu Natal, as some claimed, or had he infiltrated these gunrunning operations on behalf of the secret secret service? Is there a secret secret service in the 'new' South Africa? Does the new democratic government need a new secret service to spy on the old secret service? Is this what a new, fragile and democratic government needs to protect itself? Does one half of the secret service know what the other half of the secret service is doing? After McBride's arrest, the newspapers were full of these speculations.

When Colin Chauke, former Umkhonto We Sizwe commander, was arrested and accused of masterminding the bank heists that were plaguing Johannesburg, our amazement was complete. Were members of MK, the former guerrilla army, now putting their skills to work robbing banks?

Colin Chauke seemed extraordinary. This former guerrilla, while held in jail on suspicion of masterminding the heists, managed to retain his connection with senior government ministers, the then chief of police, and other senior members of the new government. Although he was the country's most high profile prisoner, he still managed to escape from a closely guarded jail. While on the run from the law, he lived the glamorous high life, apparently partying with cabinet ministers, buying townhouses, exotic cars and fancy clothes, and moving with seeming ease in and out of the country. After he was finally re-arrested, his girlfriend, who shared his high life, seemed unable to produce a small amount for bail or even the rent for her flat in Nelspruit. Where was all the money?

All these characters inflamed the imagination. Could the turns of their lives, so emblematic, so revelatory, be fictionalised? Could these extraordinary events, and their associated possible meanings, be made into theatre? What was it about these three figures that felt so compelling – so central to the tensions and contradictions of post-apartheid South Africa?

Was it possible that Junction Avenue Theatre Company was ready to start a new workshop?

Junction Avenue Theatre Company's mission had always, since its inception in 1976, been to make a theatre which critically reflected the conditions of apartheid South Africa. Our self-appointed task was to reveal apartheid's brutality, engage with the hidden history of struggle, and make a theatre that conscientised and polemicised. Of course, learning from Bertolt Brecht's dictum, 'A theatre that can't be laughed in, is a theatre to be laughed at', we were very conscious of the challenge to make theatre that gave pleasure. Song, dance, humour, wit, crudity – these were some of our tools. Apartheid provided our subject.

With the transition to democracy, we were temporarily fazed. Were the political imperatives and the creative energies that our company drew on no longer available to us? With the end of apartheid, it seemed to many of us that theatre making in South Africa was in crisis; had lost its subject and purpose. For many years it did not feel possible to make a new play.

Our last entirely new work had been *Tooth and Nail* (1989)[*] and the making of that play was fraught with the political tensions of the moment. From the Italian activist, Gramsci, we had learned a phrase that seemed so fitting for South Africa at that time. 'The old is dying the new is not yet born in this interregnum a great diversity of morbid symptoms appear.' The phrase seemed so apt. Apartheid was on its last legs, yet stubbornly refused to give way. Change was just around the corner, yet seemed forever delayed. Even as senior ANC members were released from jail, activists were blowing themselves up with doctored hand grenades which we now know were provided by apartheid agents masquerading as ANC activists.

The company itself was experiencing conflict. It is very difficult to sustain a non-racial company in South Africa at the best of times; these times were the worst. The problem and challenge was compounded by a series of competing ideologies, each trying to find its voice. We were experiencing morbid symptoms at first hand. We wanted to try to reflect on all these symptoms, both in the company and in the social and political world around us, in a refreshed non-realist theatre language.

We set to work in a workshop, made *Tooth and Nail*, staged it, and fell silent for ten years!

In retrospect it seems impossible to imagine – ten years without theatre making!

Of course we were not entirely silent. In the middle of the 90s we were occupied with *Marabi*, which we staged at the Performing Arts Council of the Orange Free State, at the Grahamstown Festival, at the Market Theatre and at various festivals in Britain and the USA. But *Marabi* was not a new work; it was an extensive reworking of a work the company had first staged in 1983. Was it possible that our play making days were over? It felt that way for a long time, for what could we write about? What could we critically reflect upon?

Then the series of fraught and complex arrests described above opened up a whole new field of debate about democratic 'New South Africa'. Was it possible to make a play that reflected upon social and

---

[*] Published in *At the Junction* (WUP)

political conditions post apartheid? What was so inviting and compelling about the Mzwakhe story, the McBride saga, and the Chauke scandal was that they raised some very compelling questions. What had happened to the ideals of struggle? Who had been betrayed in the 'new' South Africa? Why do some former comrades own the banks while others are accused of robbing them? Could we make a play about a people's poet and former soldier who might or might not be working for the secret secret service? What would the play really be about?

If we think about *The Fantastical History of a Useless Man, Randlords and Rotgut, Marabi, Sophiatown,* and other plays we have made over the decades, it is clear that the central subject is life in colonial segregation and apartheid Johannesburg.

———— • ————

Johannesburg. What an extraordinary South African city; a city of creativity; a city of crime, brutality and corruption; a post-apartheid melting pot of the African continent; one of the largest cities in the world not built on a river.

Johannesburg would provide the setting; Mbuli, McBride and Chauke would provide aspects of the central character.

'Why bother to rob a bank, when you can own a bank'

This is not an original thought and in fact derives from Brecht. It is in one of the final speeches of Mac the Knife the fictional hero of *Threepenny Opera.*

The theories of Bertolt Brecht have played a very influential role in much of Junction Avenue Theatre Company's work, delivering not only an attitude to content, but also a series of ideas about form and style which have always been provocative. *Threepenny Opera,* the Brecht musical of 1928, provided a primary source of inspiration for *Love, Crime and Johannesburg.*

Many South Africans have asked us, with some trepidation, whether *Love, Crime and Johannesburg* is the story of Mzwakhe Mbuli. Our answer is resolutely 'no'. Jimmy 'Longlegs' Mangane is a fictional character, a hybrid creation drawn from the historical events surrounding the lives of Mbuli, McBride and Chauke. Jimmy 'Longlegs' Mangane's character and life events are clearly fictional amalgams of aspects of these three colourful personalities. But of much more importance to Jimmy's life story is the narrative arc of Mac the Knife.

Mac the Knife is a gangster, a figure from the underworld who tangles with his old buddy, the Chief of Police. He is in love with two women, struggles with the protective father of his wife-to-be, spends too much time in the local whorehouse and, when given the opportunity to escape from prison, gets re-arrested at the whorehouse and taken to the gallows to be hanged. At the last moment, on the occasion of the queen's coronation, he is granted a pardon. A perfect model of almost mythic proportions for the narrative we were trying to create.

The basic story line of *Love, Crime and Johannesburg* had almost written itself. Jimmy 'Longlegs' Mangane, a poet of the struggle, would have intimate connections with the new Chief of Police, Queenie Dlamini, and the new Chairman of the Bank, Lewis Matome. They would be his former comrades. Jimmy would have two girlfriends – one black, Bibi Khuswayo, one white, Lulu Levine. Bokkie Levine would be the protective father-in-law-to-be, full of anxiety and antagonism, and Bones Shibambo, the gangster from Alex, the surrogate father and Jimmy's inspiration.

Jimmy would be arrested, hold court in prison and, given the chance to escape and cross the border to Swaziland, would rather seek refuge in the arms of his lover, Bibi, in a Bruma Lake hotel. He would be re-arrested and taken back to C-Max and a life sentence. At the last moment, on the occasion of the inauguration of the third president of the new democratic republic of South Africa, there would be a general amnesty, and Jimmy 'Longlegs' Mangane would be granted a reprieve. In keeping with our previous work, much of the story would be conveyed in song designed to deliberately break into the action and provide distance.

In October 1998, we, the primary authors of the play, meeting once a week, set to work to enrich the narrative we had sketched out. From the word go, the working processes and relationships were characterised by an ease, a lightness and a celebratory quality that was to find its way into the tone, content and style of the production.

In January 1999, Phase One of the workshops began. A company of about ten people gathered in the new coffee shop at the University of the Witwatersrand Theatre. In this phase, we were inviting the members of the company to test the viability of the narrative, the resonance of the themes and the verisimilitude of the characters. To our delight we discovered that the work we were proposing seemed to resonate at a deep level. The personal, political and social issues we wished to engage with seemed to be on the minds of everyone in the company. In the best sense of the word, the work seemed popular: the company's political antennae were bristling and their creative energies were ticking.

After each workshop we would retire to write and rewrite. We were struck by two things. One, the degree to which our friends and colleagues were still so politicised and highly articulate about the city and country in which we live. They constantly fed us with new ways of thinking about crime, corruption, democracy, personal relationships, Johannesburg and the 'new' South Africa. The constant debate that takes place between the highly opinionated characters in the play is, in some way, in honour of those endless coffee and dinner table conversations. Two, no matter how outrageous and absurd the story we were creating seemed to be, the daily tale of woe and delight from the newspapers proved yet again the cliché that reality is stranger than fiction. Nothing that the imagination could invent had not already been invented by Johannesburg.

Parallel to this process was the creation of the music. We were writing lyrics and taking them, in raw form, to the irrepressible Ed Jordan. He would scrutinise them for lack of scansion, rhyme and rhythm, transform them, and from his magic fingers popular and haunting music emerged. Junction Avenue Theatre Company's more traditional methods of making music were also being used. The company would improvise endless rhythms and musical lines in African jazz workshops that would evolve into snatches of songs. Later these bits would be refined into a completed work.

In Phase Two of the workshop we took a well developed narrative and set of characters to the company who worked with us to transform the material into scenes. Each company member was instructed to inhabit a character for the course of a given exercise and to role-play a given encounter. Sometimes the actor/creators would write scenes together; sometimes they would improvise the scenes directly into a tape recorder. These scenarios were transformed into finished dialogue and playable action, and the dialogue was enriched to capture the diverse registers of Johannesburg's languages and culture. There was an intense and creative flow between the study and the workshop and a particular emphasis was placed on developing a poetic and rigorous script. We had ambitions to make a highly polished and finished work.

We have been influenced by many playwrights and theatre theorists on the question of the relationship between language, politics and power. The name 'Brecht' has been invoked many times. In the context of the making of *Love, Crime and Johannesburg*, one other in particular is worth mentioning. David Mamet, the American playwright, screenwriter and film director, can teach us much about the way in which language hides what the speaker wants to reveal and reveals what the speaker wants to hide. The way people talk, and their silences, implicates them in moral and political questions and transgressions. We wanted to capture some of these qualities in Jo'burg-speak. A great deal of our work as the primary writers was hunting for this heightened and purified language, without sacrificing the particular cadences and registers of South African speech, as given to us by the members of our multicultural workshop. In every beat and every pause, to quote the ageing gangster in the play, Bones Shibambo, we wanted something to mean something.

By April 1999 we had a first draft, which was given to Sarah Roberts, the designer, who began working on a visual environment for the production. In late May rehearsals began for our première at the Standard Bank National Festival of the Arts in Grahamstown in June and a follow-on season at the Market Theatre in Johannesburg.

We were delighted when the play received a wealth of warm critical response. Our real delight, though, was that the audiences were young, diverse and clearly engaged. We were also puzzled. We were experiencing the 'death of the author' at first hand. The play that we had so carefully crafted, word by word, became something other, something alien, as the season developed. It became the property of the audience, who received it in the most unexpected ways.

Was it really this funny? Had we set out to write a comedy? Could we have predicted that Bones Shibambo's passionate outburst against contemporary crime – a gangster's condemnation of gangsterism – would provide the moral touchstone? What was it exactly about Lulu Levine's confession, 'I know you'll think I'm mad, but I love Johannesburg', that touched audiences? How is it that a diverse South African audience knows that the concept of a secret secret service is at once absurd and feasible? We knew that the cellphone scene between the Chief of Police and Lewis Matome captured aspects of contemporary mis-communications. How could we have known that it would also come to represent the powerlessness of the supposedly powerful in face of the complex machinations of the post-apartheid state and the criminal underworld?

When we reflect on the workshop, the production process and the play's reception with some months of hindsight, one thing seems particularly striking. The entire process was infused with a sense of celebration, despite the dark subjects the play was tackling. We were celebrating Johannesburg. Johannesburg is a hard city, but it is also a wonderful and creative city for those who know how to look. Further we were celebrating the achievements of South Africa's new democracy, and most importantly, we were also celebrating a release from the intense moral burden that play making in apartheid South Africa imposed. In the context of the extraordinary achievement of the 'new' South Africa, we are granted a wonderful freedom to be critical, to be dissident, to be irreverent, to be playful.

Malcolm Purkey and Carol Steinberg
Johannesburg
September 1999

'I am an artist, a poet, a soldier of the struggle'
LINDANI NKOSI (Jimmy 'Long Legs' Mangane)

LOVE, CRIME AND
JOHANNESBURG

Out of the darkness THE COMPANY *takes to the stage. They are
a strange mixture of contemporary Johannesburg, Brecht's Europe
1928, and hints of the gangsters of the South African Fifties. The
set suggests elegant café society, but has a very hard edge, metallic
and brutal.*
THE COMPANY *sings:*

LOVE, CRIME AND JOHANNESBURG

Chorus:

Noma injani ijozi	No matter how Jozi is
Siyayithanda 'thina	We love it (Jozi)
Sohlala njalo siy' thanda	We'll stay loving it (Jozi)
Nom' injani sohlala	No matter how it is we'll
Siyathanda	Keep loving it (Jozi)

Love, crime and Johannesburg
A nasty little town
Love, crime and Johannesburg
Where all the bits are breaking down

But when the thunder showers fall
And the muck is washed away
The town is almost lovely

We almost believe that we're okay

Love, crime and Johannesburg
A nasty little town
Love, crime and Johannesburg
Where dreams are made and broken down

The heart of the town is cracking
And the road to the north is long
This goddamn city's really shitty
But the cappuccino's good and strong
Chorus:
    Noma injani ijozi …

Love, crime and Johannesburg
A nasty little town
Love, crime and Johannesburg
The place is falling down

Someone should be paid to close the old whore down
But something has gone horribly wrong
The sewerage pipes are breaking
The stock exchange is relocating
The malls are quite appalling
But the cappuccino's good and strong
Chorus:
    Noma injanji ijozi …

Love, crime and Johannesburg
A nasty little town
Love, crime and Johannesburg
The place is falling, falling down

Hijackers rolled the 4 by 4 again
They've taken all the city's cash and gone
Guns they are a-running

Drugs they are a-dealing
Streets are slowly rotting
But the cappuccino's good and strong
Chorus:
Noma injani ijozi …

Love, crime and Johannesburg (3)
iJozi!

Scene 1

A Public Square

The Chief of Police, QUEENIE DLAMINI, *ushers* JIMMY 'LONG LEGS' MANGANE *to centre stage. He is heavily chained in leg irons and handcuffs and is wearing an almost cartoon-like prisoner's outfit. In spite of this, he is still smiling charmingly.*

QUEENIE: Citizens, comrades, ladies and gentlemen of the media and the press. As the Chief of Police, champion of law and order, it is my duty to announce the arrest of Jimmy 'Long Legs' Mangane – artist of the struggle, hero of the young lions – known to you all as the people's poet!

It with triumph that I deliver to you the man behind these terrible bank heists that have plagued our city!

He, who with booming voice and sweet sweet words, gave us courage in the darkest days, now stands before you arrested! Is it not a most bitter irony!

We have no doubt that he will, in flowing and elegant verse, protest his innocence, shout foul, and claim repeatedly that he is the victim of a conspiratorial plot!

However, we have irrefutable evidence that he is guilty!

Let this be a warning to all those who wish to subvert the new democracy of South Africa! No one is above the law! Evildoers will be pursued and punished!

Jimmy 'Long Legs' Mangane, in the name of the President of

the new Democratic Republic of South Africa, in the name of our peace loving citizens, in the name of our beloved city of Johannesburg, I arrest you for dangerous and reckless behaviour – lack of respect for the lives and property of others – in short, for robbing a bank with two AK47s and a hand grenade, for the princely sum of R15 0000!

JIMMY: Madam Chief of Police, my beloved fellow South Africans, I am innocent! I protest my innocence to the stars!

Surely it is clear to all of you who know me, that I have been framed! I, who gave my all, I who suffered the greatest risk, I, who offered my life for our freedom, I, Jimmy 'Long Legs' Mangane, have been wronged!

You wonder what is going on? Believe this – all I did, I did with honour! All I did, I did for my country!

QUEENIE: Tell it to the Judge!

JIMMY: I will!

QUEENIE: You will be held in a cell in maximum security without bail until your trial.

JIMMY: Hear me! I protest my innocence! I will protest it till I die! I am an artist, a poet, a soldier of the struggle! I am not a common robber! I did not rob the bank!

QUEENIE: Xelela iJudgi!

THE COMPANY *comes forward and recites:*

WITNESS JIMMY IF YOU PLEASE

Witness if you please
A strange and telling story
The story of a people's poet
Jimmy 'Long Legs' Mangane
Witness if you would
He's accused of robbery
Fifteen thousand Rand
It all just seems quite silly
Witness if you can

4

Is the story wrong or right?
What the hell is going on?
The truth is not a pretty sight

Witness as you should
Take it home and stew
What we give is fiction
It's just not true!

Any relation to real or imaginary characters
Is just not true!

Don't believe a word you hear
It's just not true!

Every thing we say and do
It's just not true!

JIMMY: Before you take me to the cells to rot, I ask only one thing.
Let me see my Lulu and my Bibi. Let me see the ones I love.

Reprise: It's just not true!

JIMMY *is joined by* BIBI KHUSWAYO *and* LULU LEVINE, *two
most elegant and striking women.*
THE COMPANY *sings an adaptation of a well known freedom song.*

JIMMY 'LONG LEGS' SIYAMTHANDA

Jimmy 'Long Legs' Siyamthanda	We love Jimmy 'Long Legs'
Sifun' ukumenz' Inkomane	We want to make him a hero
Sifun' ukumenz' Isoja	We want to make him a soldier
Sifun' Ukumenz' Iqabane	We want to make him a comrade

Repeat.

As THE COMPANY *sings, the set is changed to reveal the Prison Cell. There is a door upstage centre, which could serve a cell or a trendy Melville café.*

All set changes should be minimal and flow with the music. A minimum of blackouts should be used.

Scene 2
The Prison Cell

LULU *storms into the cell.* JIMMY *sits on his bunk. He rises and they kiss passionately.*

LULU: Jimmy! I came as soon as I could! What have they done to you? Oh my sweetheart, my darling, my poet, what have they done to you?

JIMMY: You've got to get me out of here. How are you?

LULU: I'm devastated.

JIMMY: The toilet's not working. The food's rotten. The rats are everywhere! I've spoken to the head of the prison. They're dragging their feet! The toilet is not even covered. There's no privacy in here!

LULU: Oh my darling. I'm sorry.

JIMMY: Am I dreaming? Please tell me I'm dreaming! I can't believe this is happening to me! After all my years in the struggle!

LULU: But why are they letting you rot in here? Jimmy, what's going on?

JIMMY: Why are you asking me that? You also don't believe me? Is there no one left?!

LULU: Of course I believe you! You've been framed! I love you. I believe in you. And you love me?

JIMMY: Lulu, I can't believe it! I'm rotting in hell and you're asking me about love!

LULU: Oh Jimmy, my darling, I'm sorry.

JIMMY: Lulu, my sweetie pie, my little milky bar, you've got to get me out of this.

LULU: Am I your darling? Am I your little pet?

JIMMY: Lulu, you know I love you! You can't even ask me that question. Just get me out of here and I'll show you how much I love you. I'll marry you.

LULU: If you tell me that, I can do anything!

JIMMY: A wedding! A simcha!

LULU: What do you want me to do?

JIMMY: Go to your father.

LULU: My father? Not my father! Not again!

JIMMY: He's rich. He's got rich friends. He's got friends in high places. He's connected!

LULU: He doesn't like you, Jimmy.

JIMMY: Fuck him. You do anything to get me out of here. You scream, you break everything in the house, you smash tables, you smash chairs, you cry! Just get me out of here.

LULU: Jimmy, you know I'll do my best!

JIMMY: You'll do more than that! You know that I'm innocent ...

LULU: ... and I know that you love me!

Pause.

JIMMY: Find Bones for me.

LULU: Bones?

JIMMY: You know Bones! Bones Shibambo. Go to Alex. Find him. If anyone can get me out of here, it's Bones.

LULU: Bones, in Alex.

JIMMY: Yes.

LULU: Oh Jimmy 'Long Legs', I love you!

JIMMY: And you, my lovely Lulu, I love you too!

They kiss passionately.

Scene 3

The Office of the Chief of Police

A meeting – LEWIS MATOME, *dashing, dangerous and businesslike;* BOKKIE LEVINE, *a Johannesburg Jewish business man in his fifties; and* QUEENIE DLAMINI, *a powerful graduate of the struggle.*

LEWIS: Queenie Dlamini, new Chief of Police!

QUEENIE: Lewis Matome, new Chairman of the Bank!

LEWIS: I want you to meet Bokkie Levine, my co-chair in Business Fighting Crime!

QUEENIE: Lewis Matome, you certainly pick them! Bokkie Levine, maker of teargas for the old regime!

BOKKIE: Which the new regime is perfectly happy to buy! Queenie Dlamini, it's a pleasure to meet you!

QUEENIE: And you.

LEWIS: Bokkie is helping us enormously. He knows every little scam in the city!

QUEENIE: I'm sure he does. Your reputation precedes you, Bokkie 'Bubbles' Levine!

BOKKIE: As does yours, Queenie, 'Struggle Accounting' Dlamini!

QUEENIE: Well, let's face it, Lewis, we need all the help we can get.

BOKKIE: Okay, let's not beat around the bush! We're here to plan a campaign.

LEWIS: We're right behind you, Comrade Bokkie!

QUEENIE: Well Lewis! Where once we gathered to plan a crime, now we gather to conquer crime! Not you, Bokkie, of course.

BOKKIE: If you're talking about crime, my sweetie – I've had my fair share!

LEWIS: Gentlemen, I'm already late for my next meeting! Can we begin?

QUEENIE: Sure. Ma-Gents, take a seat.

The three sit in elegant metallic armchairs.

BOKKIE: Look – let's cut through the crap! The City is on its knees, the Rand's in the sewers, the criminals are running vilt (*wild*), and we're trying to do business here!

LEWIS: We have to have a plan!

QUEENIE: Before we make a plan, we have to know what we fighting! Who we fighting, what we fighting for!

BOKKIE: What you mean 'for'? We're fighting against! Against! Against!

LEWIS: Calm down, Bokkie – calm down!

BOKKIE [*shouting*]: I'm calm – I'm calm – I'm calm!

QUEENIE: Gentlemen, please! We have big questions! How can we tackle crime when there is so much poverty?

BOKKIE: Come on! It's not the people in poverty, it's the guys with education doing the crime!

LEWIS: The syndicates are full of Harvard MBAs!

BOKKIE: Ja, it's the guys with training in MK doing all the stuff.

LEWIS: Well, let's face it – it's just so much nicer to be a bank robber than a bank clerk!

BOKKIE: It's glamorous, it's stylish, it's full of possibility!

QUEENIE: Guys, guys, whose side you on?

LEWIS: There are no more sides, Queenie!

QUEENIE: Transition brings crime. Nothing must be taken for granted.

BOKKIE: And so?

QUEENIE: It is critical to the future of this country that we contain all these elements. Either the Mafia rules us, or we will be run by the rule of the police.

BOKKIE: The police are the Mafia, my darling!

LEWIS: On the contrary, we wish that crime was more organised.

QUEENIE AND BOKKIE: What?

LEWIS: The more crime is organised, the more the streets become calm. It's all this squabbling for territory that makes life so rough out there!

QUEENIE: What a mad idea.

LEWIS: No, Queenie, it's true. We can't afford the small players any more. The small players are the wild ones. It's the wild ones we have to get rid of. Negotiate with the big ones!

BOKKIE: Negotiate! Blow them up!

LEWIS: Come on, Bokkie! We negotiated a democracy with murderers and politicians, and we can't negotiate with a few gangsters!

BOKKIE: With all due respect, since you and your new bloody democracy, there's never been so much incompetence, filth and dirt! It's as plain as day!

QUEENIE: You bloody whining whites! We blacks walk into a dark room full of stinking apartheid corruption! We turn on the light! And you blame us for the shit!

BOKKIE: Stop whining about the past! Wake up! It's the present!

LEWIS: Come on Chiefs, we're all on the same side now, remember! Bokkie, the lady's got a point!

BOKKIE: What point?

LEWIS: How can the goddamn police do any work, when there isn't any infrastructure to take a photograph or a fingerprint! We need a business operation!

BOKKIE: Listen, Lewis, we have to face the facts. Even if the police could take a photograph or a fingerprint, they so bloody corrupt, they'd be using it for the wrong reason anyway! Solutions, Queenie! We need solutions!

QUEENIE: You want my view? Here's my view – you wanna run with the big dogs you can't piss like a puppy!

LEWS AND BOKKIE: What!

QUEENIE: You want us to take on the big dogs? We need more money!

LEWS AND BOKKIE: There is no money!

QUEENIE: Print more money!

LEWIS: Don't be a fool, Queenie! You want money you got to earn it!

QUEENIE: We gotta reform the criminal justice system.

BOKKIE: Take forever …

QUEENIE: The police are on the edge!

BOKKIE: Push them over!

QUEENIE: They need help!

BOKKIE: What you want? Aromatherapy?

QUEENIE: Arrest the corrupt policemen.

BOKKIE: We'd have no policemen left.

QUEENIE: Infiltrate the criminal world! Use our best MK soldiers.

LEWIS: They're there already!

BOKKIE: We live in the crime capital of the world! Jo'burg is the crime capital of the world!

QUEENIE: Crime is on the rise all over the world! You're in Chicago, it's better in New York! You're in New York, it's bloody wonderful in Chicago!

LEWIS: Nkosi yum! What are we doing now? iGeography?

BOKKIE: Solutions, Queenie, we need solutions!

LEWIS: Ja! Unless you deliver, we take our money elsewhere.

BOKKIE: Absolutely! Crime is threatening the new South Africa!

The music begins and the full COMPANY *comes forward and sings:*

THE SONG OF THE CHIEF OF POLICE

Chorus:

Ngek' alunge	She won't manage
Lo' mthwa' unzima (2)	The load is too much

How long can a woman be a chief of police?
They don't really want a woman running the show
But the new Constitution just slipped the notion through

Chorus:

Ngek' alunge ...

How long can a woman be a chief of police?
The situation has me in a muddle
With half of these gangsters are my comrades from the struggle?

Chorus:

Ngek' alunge ...

How long can a woman be a chief of police?
Who can resist the invasion of a bank?
Piles and piles of money, we've got ourselves to thank!

Chorus:

Ngek' alunge ...

How long can a woman be a chief of police?
They say that times are changing from a woman's point of view
But everything I do must be double good and true

11

And what with the price of bread
and the monthly bill of the cellphone
We have to do what we have to do
We've been robbed right to the bone

How long can a woman be the chief of police?
QUEENIE: Not long!

Scene 4

The Prison Cell.

Before JIMMY *knows it,* BONES SHIBAMBO *is in the cell.* BONES *is a large gangster of a man, in his late fifties. He wears a suit that comes straight out of Sophiatown.*

BONES: Jimmy, my leitie! (*my youngster!*)
JIMMY: Papa Bones!
The two men dance a ritual greeting.
BONES: Jimmy 'Long Legs' Mangane!
JIMMY: Papa Bones!
BONES: Jimmy, my tsotsi! (*my ganster!*)What's my motto, my leitie?
BONES AND JIMMY: … dom dink (*dumb thinking*) and blunders is
    never my policy!
They chuckle.
BONES: In tooge se dai *(In the old days)* in the days of Saratoga
    where the birds flew backwards, brains and brawn?
JIMMY: They not buddies!
BONES: Dom dink and blunders?
JIMMY: Never, never my policy!
BONES: Kom, sit! *(Come sit!)*
BONES *and* JIMMY *sit*
BONES: What are you, a fool? What are you doing here? My slim
    sharp leities slaap nie in die tronk nie! *(My smart youngsters don't
    sleep in jail!)*
JIMMY: Baba Bones, you know I'm not guilty!

BONES: Guilty or not guilty – here you sit wearing a badge of prisoner! Is this what I taught you?

JIMMY: Bones …

BONES: I taught you honour, style, professionalism! And now! In die tronk! The top of the body stays the brain, below the navel, Emzanza Afrika, *(Below Africa)* you find the land of temptation and blunders!

JIMMY: This has nothing to do with my Sqeezas, Baba! *(My girlfriends, Father)*

BONES: Don't you call me Baba! Am I your flesh and blood? No! And now you just a moegoe! *(stupid fool)*

JIMMY: Sorry, Baba!

BONES: If you got a puppy, and it's got a worm, you take the worm out! Am I right?

JIMMY: Baba, you're right!

BONES: When you were a puppy, you got a sex worm, and I never managed to get it out!

JIMMY: DiBones, I've been framed!

BONES: Masipa, man! *(Shit, man)*

JIMMY: It's true!

BONES: Politics het gekom en het verby, die Luthulis, en die Jan Smuts, en al daa'ie kak. April '94 het gekom, Mandela het gekom, en die hele wêreld het gedans.

(Politics came and politics went, the Luthulis and the Jan Smuts, and all that shit, April '94 came, Mandela came, and the whole world danced)

Ek het onder gesit, gekyk en gedink! *(I sat down and looked and thought)*

Ek het nie van die wêreld gedink, ek het van die soul gedink, my well being! Wie is ek?

(I didn't think of the world, I thought of my soul, my well being! Who am I?)

Right through the days of politics, van apartheid af tot amandla, niks het gechange! Nothing changed! Die beste, die beste on your side is – jy's goed met die wat jy ken. Good at what you know! Good at what you are!

(Right through the days of politics, from apartheid to power,
Nothing changed! The best, the best is on your side – You're
good at what you know! Good at what you are!)

JIMMY: I'm good, DiBones! I'm good!

BONES: You're committed! You're a poet. You're a fighter. Why
are you here? Jy het jou favourites. *(You've got your favourites).*
Cherries, politics, sport, die kak poetry ding! *(Girls, politics,*
sport, this shit poetry thing!) Maar die important ding *(but the*
important thing) – look bloody after yourself – tough love, my
leitie … lewe jou lewe in die beste way vat ek het jou gevuis!
(Live your life in the best way that I showed you!)

Haii bamba haii luma. Jy was a hero van die struggle. Ja, die
beste groot mond … die beste rap en al daii gemors! Nou, jy
dink elke mense owes you! No one owes you a thing! Favours,
kak! You are the same leitie I taught! Wake up and look after
your self, vuka! Suga, word vakke, ga gona kgomo ya boroko,
man! You've lost your golden touch!

(No holding, no biting. You were a hero of the struggle. Yes, the
best big mouth … the best rap and all that mess! Now, you think
every man owes you! No one owes you a thing! Favours, shit!
You are the same young guy I taught! Wake up and look after
yourself, wake up, wake up, wake up! You go to a cow for milk,
not sleep, man!)

JIMMY: Baba Bones, you're being unfair! They arrested me!

BONES: You're an embarrassment! They're laughing at you in the
streets! Can't pull a simple bank job!

JIMMY: I told you! I'm innocent!

BONES: Sure! The jails are full of innocent men! First rule of the
game – don't get caught!

JIMMY: They put guns in my car! They put guns in my boot!

BONES: Who?

JIMMY: You know they been trying to kill me…

BONES: Who!

JIMMY: I don't know who…

BONES: Aah! bullshit! What have you learnt? You've learnt nothing!

JIMMY: You're my father! You're my inspiration…

BONES: Where's the money?

JIMMY: Stop talking about the money!

BONES: Waars die kunene? Waars die chee? Waars die mazuma? Chee, chelete! Kanupe amagoa, man! *(Where's the money? Where's the llule buttons, man!)*

JIMMY: I told you! I don't have any money!

BONES: You don't get it, do you? This town runs on money. No money, no quick walk to freedom! You think I can get you out without money?

JIMMY: You just won't listen, will you!

BONES: Kom, Jimmy! Dis Johannesburg, man! Die whele loop op geld! *(Come, Jimmy! This is Johannesburg, man! The wheels run on money!)* You so busy with you poetry and your poes, *(puss)* man, that you forgotten to take a close look at the book of life! Times are changed, Jimmy, you not the hero and the poet any more, you just some lousy bank robber, and you can't even get that right!

JIMMY: I did not rob the bank!

BONES: Luister my Leitie, *(Listen my youngster)* the underworld is the underworld, is the underworld. My life's the same as it always was. New South Africa, Old South Africa, who gives a damn? Don't get me wrong, I love our new President. A genius! A miracle! But how's my life changed? I'm still making my way in the gutters. I survive the same way as I always did. No one makes things happen for me.

So you made a fuck up, they say you got only fifteen thousand, you say you didn't do it – lets put those questions aside, how we gonna get you out of here? Jimmy use your head, use the lessons I taught you when you were on my knee. We gonna spring you – we gonna get a key! We gonna get these gates open! We gonna take the long walk to freedom! Just tell me where's the real money!

JIMMY: There is no real money!

BONES: Voetsak, man! *(Bugger off, man!)* Either you kak stupid beyond stupid, or you're a bloody liar!

Scene 5

A City Council Boardroom

LULU, *dressed in a male suit, pin striped and beautifully cut, makes a presentation to an imaginary Greater City Council.*

LULU: Think of Johannesburg. Greater Johannesburg. South of Soweto, from Orange Farm to the border of Midrand in the north. The place looks like a kidney, like a sort of squashed kidney. Think of the M1 north. Think of the east. Benoni, Brakpan, Boksburg. Think of the great cities of the world. Rome, Paris, Beijing, Buenos Aires, London, New York, Johannesburg!

Johannesburg is the largest city in the world not built on a river!

This is why we're mad! This is why the city is crazy! We need water!

Madam chair, city councillors, Central City Solutions propose the following – we are going to change the M1 into a river and replace Benoni, Boksburg and Brakpan with a sea!

Our consulting engineers assure us that all entrances to the M1 can be easily dammed up and with a few minor pumps we can make the river flow all the way to Pretoria.

To tell you the truth, we're not really sure which city is lower – Jo'burg or Pretoria – but this, I'm assured by the engineers is a minor detail.

You know the sea at Sun City? How it waves and crashes? We've been told by the engineers that we can create about thirty or forty of those and nobody will ever know it's man made.

Unfortunately moving Benoni, Boksburg and Brakpan is a little harder!

THE COMPANY *sings*:

GAUTENG

Gauteng Go monate (3)   It's lovely in Gauteng
Go monate mo Gauteng

16

Ditsotsi tsa mo a di sa dlala	Tsotsis don't gamble with
ma- dice	dice any more
Di rpoa di banka di bolaya batho	They rob banks and kill people
Maginsta ka dithunya le di car hijack	Guys with guns and car hijacking
House breaker, jack roller	
House breaker, jack roller,	
Tshaba di fedile	The nation is finished

Mo Gauteng

Gauteng Go monate (3)
Go monate mo Gauteng

To stroll at night is to take a risk
They break your back and empty your pockets
Boys and girls, it's just the same

Scene 6
The Prison Cell

BIBI is pacing up and down. She is dressed to the nines, a startlingly original creation. Fake leopard skin abounds.

BIBI: Ay Lolo, I bumped into George in Sandton as I was on my way to the cellphone shop. My cellphone is giving so much crap! Awuyazi nawe lama Nokia, aish (*You know how these things [Nokias] are*) … I must just get myself an Ericsson!

Anyway, so I bumped into George and he's got himself a new girlfriend – ithi ngikutshele (*let me tell you*).

JIMMY: A new girlfriend!

BIBI: I don't know where he picks them up! Fake jewellery, fake nails, fake teeth and the biggest pair of fake boobs I've ever seen!

So, anyway, George asked me if they've granted you bail and how much. As if he was gonna put up the money!

JIMMY: George!

BIBI: Yaz (*Gee*), some people bayathandu khubukisa (*they like to show off*), they just like to show off in front of their girlfriends! I'm sure he was just boasting that he knew you!

JIMMY: Ai, man!

BIBI: Bengidinwe (*I was so irritated*)! Ai, I was so irritated, my God! So, I left there and next thing I don't even go to that cellphone shop. Next thing ngayafika (*I end up at*) iGucci, I see this bag that I must just own! Oh Jimmy, it's so beautiful. I wish ungiyaibona, ine snake skin, or … maybe iOstrich, nje the material lenaprints leshing … ngathi icathulo zika Vusi Khumalo (*I wish you could see it, it is made of snake skin, or maybe ostrich, like the material that has prints, like Vusi Khumalo's shoes*). You know his shoes? The ones he loves to wear when he goes to the jazz clubs? So anyway, when the cashier said it was five thousand, I just paid for it without thinking twice. Now, Lolo, my darling, my problem, nje, is just the rent. I've got money but I'm a little short!

JIMMY: Exactly how little short are we talking here?

BIBI: Lolo, sthandwa sami, my love, yazi kutough outside now! They want to evict now, and those people be-fridge (*furniture people*) were there, I don't know. Uyaz?

JIMMY: Bibi! Ufuna? (*How much?*) How much? How much do you need?

BIBI: Aagh shame, Sthandwa, don't worry. I'll try and ask uMandla to loan us and then uzobetaala (*you'll pay him back*) when you get out.

JIMMY: No, no! I'll make a plan. Just tell me how much you need.

BIBI: Mina aish angazi, (*Me, hey, I don't know*). But if you could just give me for the rent and, well, the cellphone account, and pay for the fridge and the microwave to stay … oh, ja (*yes*), and there's no groceries in the house.

JIMMY: Ja, okay, I'll make some phone calls!

BIBI: Aii, Jimmy …!

JIMMY: Bibi, don't worry, everything will be fine by tomorrow.

BIBI: Ay, Lolo! Thank you, my sweetheart! If only they knew how much we're struggling, they'd never accuse you of robbing banks!

JIMMY: Bibi, I love you.

BIBI: Oh Lolo, I love you too!

JIMMY: When I'm a proper gentleman, I'll marry you.

BIBI: Oh Lolo, If you become a proper gentleman, I'll no longer love you!

JIMMY comes forward and sings. On the one side of the stage, in the shadows, stands BIBI, on the other, LULU.

JIMMY'S SONG

I love my Bibi and I love my Lulu
I love my canvas brown and pink
I love to paint them with my colours
To splash them till we sigh and sink

Lulu is so pure so sweet
When I'm with her I'm an angel
Bibi is my love potion
When I'm with her I can paint the ocean

To etch myself upon them is my veritable delight.
How the pink canvas catches the light
How the brown reveals the shades of white!

Some days I need to rub against the rough
Some days I need I need to rest upon the smooth
I need my palate complete
I need to be loved from my ears to my feet! (3)

Scene 7

Bokkie's Study

He's making a fool of you, Lulu!'
GINA SHMUKLER AND LAWRENCE JOFFE (Bokkie 'Bubbles' Levine)

LULU: Daddy, you've got to help me get Jimmy out of prison.

BOKKIE: Lulu, my shnookums, what the hell can I do?

LULU: You've got connections. You're a big wig in the town.

BOKKIE: So?

LULU: Get a favour out of Lewis Matome.

BOKKIE: Matome? He's just a business man!

LULU: Daddy, You know as well as I do, your friend Lewis Matome is a powerful man!

BOKKIE: So?

LULU: He's in with the big boys! He's close to the ear of the President!

BOKKIE: If you really wanna know – the only thing closer to the President's ear is the President's ear wax!

LULU: That's my point!

BOKKIE: And so?

LULU: He's your big chaver *(friend)*! He can help get Jimmy out!

BOKKIE: If you really wanna know, I 'm glad your poet is in prison!

LULU: Daddy, how can you say that!

BOKKIE: Because I believe it!

LULU: Jesus!

BOKKIE: I don't want you to see that gangster friend of yours any more! He's a danger! Besides – he writes kak poetry! I know this is the new South Africa but there are limits!

LULU: You always said your greatest happiness is my happiness!

BOKKIE: And so?

LULU: I'm your princess, your precious, your blessing...

BOKKIE: And so?

LULU: Daddy, I'm so unhappy, I can't live without him!

BOKKIE: You're in love with a shwartsa *(black)*!

LULU: Daddy ...

BOKKIE: And what's more, not just any shwartsa – a gangster shwartsa!

LULU: That is not a nice word!

BOKKIE: I didn't send you to an expensive Jewish day school so that you could end up in love with a shwartsa!

LULU: That's where I met him, remember!

BOKKIE: I've forgotten. Remind me!

LULU: Jesus! Jews for Social Justice.

BOKKIE: Oi vay!

LULU: He's a great artist of the struggle and a proper mench. So leave me alone. It's thanks to heroes like Jimmy that we're free today. Where were you in the days of struggle?

BOKKIE: Paying for your education and your nice clothes and your mother's psychiatric bills. Which CV do you want to see?

LULU: Making razor wire for the apartheid regime!

BOKKIE: Which the new regime is fully happy to buy! I'm a standing member of the ANC and a trustee of the President's what-dja-ma-call-it fund! 250 000 big ones buys me the ear of the head of state at the drop of an earring! Whose ears you got?

LULU: Daddy! The man I love is rotting in prison!

BOKKIE: If you want to see your precious poet – you see me no

21

more! Don't you know that he's having a love affair with another woman? He's making a fool of you, Lulu!

LULU: Rubbish! You would say anything to turn me against him!

BOKKIE: Open your eyes, Girlie. You want to know where she is? She's just a gun-shot away! She hangs out at the Paradise Café.

LULU: Rubbish! Not true! First the state frames him, now you're framing him! He's been framed twice!

BOKKIE: Her name is Bibi, and if you don't believe me, go and find her!

Scene 8

The Prison Cell

Lewis comes through the door, reciting some of JIMMY's *poetry.*

LEWIS: I am the river that flows through Africa!
    I am the ancient source
    I am memory and history
    Past and future
    I am the river that flow through Africa!

JIMMY: Comrade Lewis!

LEWIS: Comrade Jimmy!

JIMMY: Or should I say Mister Matome?

LEWIS: Jimmy, my brother.

JIMMY: What are you doing here? You're the last person I expected to see. You, the Chairman of the Bank. Me, the bank robber. What do you want, Mr. Matome?

LEWIS: Help me and I'll help you. You crossed the line, comrade.

JIMMY: Whose fucking line?

LEWIS: Be reasonable, Jimmy.

JIMMY: What you doing here? Sniffing for the truth! Who for? The Chief of Police? The President? The head of National Intelligence?

LEWIS: Did you rob the bank, Jimmy? Why did you rob the bank, Jimmy?

JIMMY: Listen Lewis, I don't have to answer to you, I answer to the people.

LEWIS: Cut the crap, Jimmy!

JIMMY: Why am I having to ask favours from you? We were in this thing together at the start. In the struggle! Right through the darkest days! Why didn't we finish together? Here you are right at the top of the dung hill. And I'm in the shit hole! I read in the paper, you're worth forty million.

LEWIS. Sure.

JIMMY: Why you? What did you do different to me? We were comrades! Cadres! We were brothers in arms!

LEWIS: You just don't get it, do you? Things changed. There's a new set of rules to play by now. I ran with the ball. You sat on your gat waiting for hand-outs. Then you get bitter and you rob my bank.

JIMMY: The problem with you lot at the top of the dung hill – you think you smell like roses. You come in here, you offer me a deal. I call it blackmail. Well maybe two can play that game. Either you help me, or I look elsewhere for help!

LEWIS: You got no cards left to play, Jimmy. You're in jail.

JIMMY: If I did rob your bank – and I'm not saying I did – but if I did rob the bank, at least it was just a bank. You robbed the people.

LEWIS: Me? Me?

JIMMY: You ride in on the back of the struggle and what do you do? You suck the lifeblood out of all of us. In the name of all that's good and pure, you got rich!

LEWIS: Tell it to your mother, Jimmy …

JIMMY: So, if I did rob the bank, and I'm not saying I did, but if I did rob the bank, I was just taking back some of what you stole from the rest of us.

LEWIS: No one took anything from you. You think the world owes you a favour. No one cares what you did before.

JIMMY: Rubbish!

LEWIS: Read my lips. There is no past!

JIMMY: What you saying!

LEWIS: There is no history! There is no past! There is no right and wrong. It's a whole new world. And now you rob a lousy bank!

JIMMY: I was just repossessing what was mine.

LEWIS: Don't be a fool, Jimmy, that kind of talk gets you nowhere.

JIMMY: And you? First a comrade, now the owner of all the banks!

The music breaks into the action. THE COMPANY *comes forward.*
There is a hint of the barricades.

LEWIS'S SONG OF CAPITAL

LEWIS: Of course we must take over
    The commanding heights of capital
    We are needed in South Africa
    To rule the mines and precious metal
THE COMPANY: Aaah, Aaah
LEWIS: We must take the reins of boardrooms
    It's our struggle and our call
    Own the banks – own the banks
    Do we want the whites to run them all?
Chorus:
    Own the banks, own the banks
    Own the banks, own the banks
    This is our struggle and our call
    Do we want the whites to own them all?
LEWIS: When the word came from the president
    I rose up to the challenge
    Someone had to heed the call
    Show me another
    Who has the balls!
THE COMPANY: He has big balls!
LEWIS: Every man to do his duty
    Even if it is unfair
    We know the job is really shitty
    But this way lies our market share
Chorus:
    Own the banks, own the banks …
The mood changes considerably.
LULU: Where's your old commitment?
    We used to see your courage
    Fighting on the barricades
ALL: Where's your old commitment?

LULU: You used to fight for justice
   Now you sweat for your bank statement
LEWIS: Patience my dear Lulu
   Times are hard
   The Rand is gasping
   Someone needs to take the reigns and fly
ALL: Fly – y – y
LEWIS: Who better than a comrade
   To know that life's a bitch
   A soldier trained in struggle
   We must get –
ALL : Stinking rich!
   Own the banks (4)
   We – must – get – stinking – rich!

Scene 9

A Melville Café

LULU sits pensively nursing a drink. She addresses the audience.

LULU: I know you'll think I'm mad, but I love Johannesburg.
   Johannesburg keeps me on my toes. I take nothing for granted
   here. Everything I ever thought, I have to think it fresh here.
   Everything I ever imagined, I have to turn it on its head. I am
   loving Johannesburg! Wild city! Damned city! City of every
   pleasure and every pain!

   This madness, this blood! I can't imagine living anywhere
   else. It's so ugly, it's so brutal. There is so little out there, I'm
   forced to turn in on my own heart.

   My Johannesburg heart! There I find a tenderness I never
   believed possible. My heart is like Johannesburg. A wound. It's
   raw, it's bloody, alive to every possibility.

Scene 10
Office of the Chief of Police

QUEENIE *sits.* JIMMY *stands, handcuffed and chained.*

QUEENIE: What do you want to see me for, Jimmy?

JIMMY: Come on Queenie, we're old friends.

QUEENIE: You know it's difficult for me.

JIMMY: What do you mean?

QUEENIE: How do you think it looks if I'm seen fraternising with the accused?

JIMMY: Queenie, let's cut the crap. Let's make a deal.

QUEENIE: What can you offer me, Jimmy?

JIMMY: What do you need, Queenie?

QUEENIE: Okay. Let's say I need to know who's crossed the line.

JIMMY: What do mean?

QUEENIE: Which of our comrades, have crossed the line!

JIMMY: What you mean, Queenie, crossed the line?

QUEENIE: You know what I mean!

JIMMY: Do you mean taking a bribe … taking some land cheap … selling off a game park … employing your girlfriend/boyfriend?

QUEENIE: I want to know, which of our soldiers is doing the bank heists.

JIMMY: How would I know?

QUEENIE: Oh come on, Jimmy!

JIMMY: If I do know – and I'm not saying I do know – but if I do know and I tell you, what are you going to do for me, Madame Chief of Police?

QUEENIE: Here's the deal, Jimmy. Get me stuff I can use and I'll get you a lighter sentence.

JIMMY: Fuck your lighter sentence! I'm out of here or no deal!

QUEENIE: You've got no cards to play, Jimmy.

Silence

JIMMY: You want the secret, I'll tell you the secret. The President can't trust the secret service.

QUEENIE: What do you mean?

JIMMY: You know as well as I do.

QUEENIE: No I don't.

JIMMY: What does the President do when he needs quality information? Information he can believe?

QUEENIE: What do you mean?

JIMMY: Well say guns are running from Mozambique to KwaZulu-Natal. Who's running the guns from Mozambique to KwaZulu-Natal? Explosives taken to Cape Town? Who's taking explosives to Cape Town? Someone's bombing the police stations. Who's bombing the police stations?

QUEENIE: It's my job to know this stuff!

JIMMY: And do you know it, Queenie?

Silence

JIMMY: My point exactly. So, what does the President do? The President sets up a secret secret service.

QUEENIE: What?

JIMMY: A secret service inside the secret service.

QUEENIE: You've lost me, Jimmy.

JIMMY: A secret service set up to keep an eye on the secret service. A hand-picked group of highly trusted individuals.

QUEENIE: And where do you fit into this?

JIMMY: I'm right inside, Queenie.

QUEENIE: Is that so?

JIMMY: I'm a valuable, trusted, chosen member.

QUEENIE: If you're right inside, and if this whole song and dance is true – and I'm not saying I believe it's true, then what are you doing sitting here! Chained and handcuffed, rotting in jail?

JIMMY: If the President had a secret secret service, would he admit he had a secret secret service? That would be disaster! Admit all this and our precious New South Africa falls apart!

QUEENIE: All this still doesn't explain why you were caught red-handed robbing a bank.

JIMMY: Must I spell it all out to you? I was on a special assignment to infiltrate the gangs. Some of your best buddies, Queenie, they in there up to their eyeballs!

QUEENIE: What are you saying, Jimmy?

JIMMY: Who better than a trained guerilla to penetrate the bank vaults with military precision? Who better than a trained guerilla to throw chains across the roads? Who better to bribe and corrupt? Who knows the underground path better than the freedom fighter? And besides, who's pissed off and unemployed in this precious New South Africa?

QUEENIE: It's a good story, Jimmy.

JIMMY: I was working for the secret secret service. I was infiltrating the criminal crowd. I got caught. Now they have to deny me. Three times they spit upon my grave. The bastards!

Scene 11
The Open Door

The stage becomes very dark. A piercing light reveals BONES *standing in the doorway. He talks directly to the audience.*

BONES: Me. You wanna know about me? I am outraged! Gatvol! My heart is full of anger! Ke tlhaguna magala a mahibidu. Ke nkga masepa ka molomo. *(I chew red hot coal. I am so angry all that comes out of my mouth smells like shit.)*

    Who are these people? They lock their victims in meat fridges – suffocate them to death! They take hot irons and iron people's faces! They rape eighty-year-old ladies! Ba sule maikutlo. Dipelo di thatafetse. *(Their feelings are dead. Their hearts have turned to stone.)* Where is the honour, where is the style, what has happened to the profession? Full of riff raff and violent little boys!

    In the old days, toeka se dae, we were proper gangsters, bo dimane. We had a set of rules, a code of conduct! Ons het die Capos, die kingpins geluister. *(We listened to the chiefs, the kingpins.)* There were certain ways and means we did things! We knew who we were robbing and why! We didn't want blood. Die moegoes is bloody vampires! *(These fools are bloody vampires).* We didn't want bullet holes through the head. We used reason! Everybody's too greedy now. Onse motto *(our motto)* was small amounts, pride and cleanliness in our work! And full amount of honour! Now, they just mad! These young boys. They kill for nothing! They like to hear the screaming! They're bloody vampires!

We went to church schools. We learnt respect. We fed our children, looked after our mothers.

Them! Their mothr gun, fast car, easy money and lots of poes! No school, no family, no God!

They dunno who they are! No balls, nothing inside! They gotta do all this stuff so they feel like men! Burning, suffocating, raping, shooting! Ek is vokken gatvol! (*I am bloody fed up! Guts full!*) So if you want to know about Jo'burg, kwa nyama ayipheli – kuphela amazinyo endoda, kwa nyama ayipheli – kuphela amazinyo endoda (lit: *there's so much meat in Jo'burg that you cannot finish it – only the man's teeth will deteriorate*; fig: *lots to see and do in Jo'burg – you'll never manage it all*). Joeys … Egoli … Jozi-Jozi – I say, break it all up – start again!

Scene 12
The Prison Cell

LEWIS *comes through the door. He is still reciting some of* JIMMY's *poetry.*

LEWIS: I am the river that flows through Africa!
    I am the rock and the desert sand
    I am the broken chain
    Forged in the bitter fire
    I am the river that flow through Africa!
JIMMY: Back again, Lewis?
LEWIS: Just a friendly visit, Jimmy.
JIMMY: Just a friendly visit!
LEWIS: Sure, a friendly, friendly visit.
JIMMY: Oh, come on, Lewis! A friendly visit to a bank robber?
LEWIS: Queenie's getting agitated, Jimmy.
JIMMY: And so?

LEWIS: You know how that woman can talk.

JIMMY: Aagh!

LEWIS: Why you upsetting the Chief of Police, Jimmy? What you telling her?

JIMMY: I'm telling her nothing!

LEWIS: Come on, Jimmy.

JIMMY: Listen, I'm telling her what she knows already!

LEWIS: Well, then, it seems she doesn't know that she knows it!

JIMMY: Lewis, I'm in jail, I'm accused of bank robbery. I got no cards to play.

LEWIS: You're seeing the Chief of Police!

JIMMY: I'm seeing Queenie Dlamini! Why is that upsetting you, Lewis?

LEWIS: Every time you talk to the Chief of Police, she goes squealing to her people.

JIMMY: And so?

LEWIS: There are just some things, Jimmy, the cops just don't need to know.

JIMMY: Ayi, suga … (*Hey, bugger off …*)

LEWIS: People are getting upset, Jimmy.

JIMMY: Which people?

LEWIS: People you need on your side.

JIMMY: No-one's on my side, Lewis! I'm on my own. You guys are leaving me with no option.

LEWIS: You're not being sensible, Jimmy.

JIMMY: Listen, if I rot in jail you all coming down with me! Put that in your pipe and smoke it! I'm not gonna be anybody's martyr!

LEWIS: Nobody wants you rotting in jail, Jimmy. We're working on a plan.

JIMMY: What you got in mind, Lewis?

LEWIS: Stop talking to Queenie, and start talking to Lewis, Jimmy. You gotta tell me all you know.

JIMMY: How do I know that if I tell you what I know, you not gonna tell it to the wrong people?

LEWIS: Listen Jimmy, you talking to me, Lewis Matome. Have you forgotten? My people are not the wrong people!

JIMMY: You get me out of here, and I'll tell you what you need to know.

LEWIS: You pushing it, Jimmy! You gotta give me something to work on!

JIMMY: The African Bird can only truly sing when he is free!

LEWIS: Oh fuck me! Poetry!

THE COMPANY *sings a reprise as they change the set.*

Scene 13
A Melville Café

BIBI: Hi.

LULU: Hi.

BIBI: You're Lulu.

LULU: And you must be Bibi.

BIBI: Of course.

BIBI *mutters under her breath.*

LULU: Sorry?

BIBI: I was just saying, you're more beautiful than I ever thought you could be!

LULU: Well, you seem rather a handful yourself.

BIBI: Lulu Levine.

LULU: Bibi … Bibi …

BIBI: Khuswayo!

LULU: Funny, he never mentioned you.

BIBI: Awuzwe lesishwapha … *(Listen to this piece of rag)*

LULU: uThini? *(You said?)*

BIBI: Nothing …

LULU: Don't you think Yeoville is still so interesting?

BIBI: Not really …

LULU: You know during the struggle we often used to meet in Yeoville.

BIBI: Well, the closest I've ever been to the struggle is trying to work out how to have sex with the whole of Pirates and Chiefs – before *The Bold and the Beautiful*!

LULU: Pathetic!

BIBI: Just kidding!

LULU: I think it's time to order.

BIBI: Yes.

LULU AND BIBI: Cappuccino!

LULU: Look, let's not beat around the bush. We have a problem. Jimmy's in jail, and we have to find a way to get him out.

BIBI: What do you think we can do together that I can't do by myself!

LULU: Look, I have lots of connections.

BIBI: And so?

LULU: Well, I think you have lots of skills.

BIBI: What do you mean?

LULU: Well. Do you know Lewis Matome?

BIBI: Of course! Lewis Matome, the new Chairman of the Bank!

LULU: Lewis is one of the most powerful men in the city.

BIBI: And so?

LULU: Well, I thought we could try and seduce him.

BIBI: What do you mean?

LULU: Well to be frank, I thought you could try and seduce him.

BIBI: Are you mad!

LULU *is on the retreat.*

LULU: Relax!

BIBI: He's sleeping with half the women in town already and no one gives a damn!

LULU: Oh…

BIBI: And you want to know who cares the least? His wife!

LULU: Well. Jiimmy, when I saw him, said I should contact a friend of his in Alex.

BIBI: Who?

LULU: Bones.

BIBI: Bones? Bones Shibambo, the old gangster?

LULU: Yes.

BIBI: Please, what could he do to help? He's past it! He's just a has-been!

LULU: Well, what have you got to offer?

BIBI: Maybe we can flood the courts? The comrades still love him.

LULU: We've got to get him out, we really have to get him out!

BIBI: I didn't realise how much you care for him. Look, this is a state of emergency! Once he's out, I'll let you see him once or twice – before we get married.

LULU: How could you possibly think that he wants to marry you?

BIBI: He's already proposed, sweetheart! Three times.

LULU: What on earth do you think you could offer Jimmy? Besides he's already committed to marrying me!

BIBI: Tixo! (*Oh my God!*) How you could possibly think he would want to marry you! I know about you women, you just lie there, motionless – intellectual – cold …

LULU: Sensitive! Caring! And loving! And besides I understand him as a man!

BIBI: You don't understand him as a man! I understand him as a man! Look at me – this is what a man wants! You're just Jimmy's meal ticket! Once we get him out of jail, he's going to make a career in Government and then all will be fine.

LULU: Jimmy loves me! He's always loved me! He might have loved you when he was young, but he's left all that behind! Don't you understand? He's a sophisticated man now. We share a vision, we share a sense of the future!

BIBI: Jimmy loves you about as much as one loves an *Oxford English Dictionary*! You might have been useful to him once, but he doesn't need all that stuff any more! He loves me.

LULU: He loves me!

BIBI: He loves me!

LULU: He loves me!

BIBI: He loves me!

The two women sing a duet.

I STAND BY MY MAN

BIBI *and* LULU: As the cool evening comes
    As the dark follows me
    I will pray to the powers
    Set him free

    Let the wind rush on in
    Blow away all his sin
    Back to where we begin
    Back with me
Chorus:
    And I will stand by my man
    Do all that I can
    To let him know he's never alone
    I won't stop till he's free
    'cause then he'll be loving me
    'cause he is mine I won't let him go
    No, I won't let him go

    He'll be cruel to be kind
    He'll be kind to be cruel
    Yet I give him my soul
    I'm a fool

    It's the power of need
    Drives me slowly insane
    Will the medicine man
    Come and ease my pain
Chorus :
    And I will stand by my man …

    It's my time to be strong
    It's my time to believe
    Come on show me a sign
    That it is me you need

Can you listen to her
When you know what I do
I will give up my life
For the love of you

Chorus :
And I will stand by my man ...

Scene 14

A Melville Café.

LEWIS *comes forward and addresses the audience. He is at his most suave and charming.*

LEWIS: Yes, yes, yes, if you want more of this R & B, go to Melville! Jazz at Jabulani at the Hyatt, Kwela and Kwaito at Wandies in Soweto. Blues wherever you look! Saturday in Jo'burg. Bliss!

Be careful! Johannesburg has a reputation for violent crime! But it is also has the friendliest, most interesting people in South Africa! It's the most cosmopolitan and fastest moving metropole in the Southern hemisphere!

Jo'burg! A city unlike any other in Africa. It has the wealthiest, most sophisticated and liberal thinking population on the continent!

Imagine! Frothy Cappuccino at the Belem in downtown Johannesburg, with thick Portuguese sweet pastries! A detour to the old Mai Mai migrant workers' market to stock up on trendy Zulu tyre sandals, Mbanthanda!

Sushi and chilled wine at a Parkhurst pavement café!

Later, Indian roti and curry in Fordsburg for dinner! Saturday in Jo'burg – Bliss!

Take a walk on the wild side!

On crowded township streets! Over there – small kraals of goats and chickens; over there – wedding cakes and coffin manufacturers; over there – hairdressers tending to their clients

under trees! This here, Mankhukhu – Mandela Village!
Everything permeated with the smell of atjar and magwenya!
Ah, Jo'burg, glorious, unforgettable Jewel of Africa!

THE COMPANY *bursts into song.*

FOR THE LOVE OF MONEY

Chorus:
Ho-lololololo	Cash, cash
Moola dough	Bread, cash, cash
Borotho banyana ba	Cash
Emjipa ejozi kukhulum Icash!	Money speaks in Jozi

LULU *and* BIBI: Can it be that there so many words
For the one thing that gives so much pleasure
We are turning our hearts into stone
For the pressures of living in leisure

Walala wena Ejozi	You sleep in Jozi
Money – re buwa ka banyana ba	We talking about money
Borotho – sikhuluma ngenyuku	Bread, we talking money
Smega – sikhala ngamapeni bo	Money, we talking about pennies
Borotho	Bread

Chorus:
Ho-lololololo …

LULU *and* BIBI: I feel like you swallow me whole
You told me with cash we'd be better
Can you honestly tell me you care
Temporarily right out of order

Scene 15

The Prison Cell

LULU *sits silently on the bunk as* JIMMY *uses all his powers of persuasion.*

JIMMY: Lulu, you must believe me. Bibi's nothing! She was my last fling, my last little flap of the old wing before I marry you! When I marry you I will be the happiest man alive. When I marry you, I am going to be the most faithful of men. How could you doubt me? Look at me and tell me you can't see a man who loves you! A man who adores you! A man who worships you! When I am married to you there will be no one who could be more faithful. It's true!

Scene 16

Office Corridors

'Do we let him out or do we keep him in?'
LINDA SEBEZO (Queenie Dlamini, Chief of Police) and Arthur Molepo

Shadows dominate, but two rather sinister pools of light are evident.
QUEENIE *is in the one,* LEWIS *is in the other. There is a significant
distance between them.*

They are both on cellphones.

QUEENIE: So? Must I keep him in, or must I let him out? I want to
know. I need to know.

LEWIS: Can we, with a clear conscience, keep him behind bars? Is
that the question?

QUEENIE: Is what the question?

LEWIS: In short and in truth, is he innocent or is he guilty?

QUEENIE: Is that the question?

LEWIS: Is he innocent or is he guilty?

QUEENIE: Damned cellphone! You're breaking up ... you're
breaking up ...

LEWIS: Hello? Hello? Are you there?

QUEENIE: I'm here, I'm here! Is that the question?

LEWIS: Is what the question?

QUEENIE: Look let's say he robbed the bank, and I'm not saying he
did, that doesn't mean he's guilty.

LEWIS: I'm losing you ...

QUEENIE: I said ... Just because he robbed the bank , doesn't mean
he's guilty ...

LEWIS: I'm losing you ...

QUEENIE: I said ... Just because ...

LEWIS: I can hear what you are saying, but what do you mean?

QUEENIE: I mean, there may be a good reason to rob a bank.

LEWIS: Come on, Queenie!

QUEENIE: No look, if he's in the secret secret service, maybe they
wanted him to rob the bank!

LEWIS: You're breaking up again!

QUEENIE: What?

LEWIS: You've gone completely fuzzy!

QUEENIE: I said, if he's in the secret secret service, maybe they
wanted him to rob the bank!

LEWIS: Oh, come on, Queenie!

QUEENIE: That's the sort of thing the secret secret service does. Take bombs to Cape Town! Infiltrate the gun running operations! Launder the money! That sort of thing! Some of our best bomb planters and gun runners have been our own guys!

LEWIS: Let's say he's innocent.

QUEENIE: I'm losing you!

LEWIS: Let's say he's innocent!

QUEENIE: Well ... let's say he's been framed, let's say the secret secret service put the money and the guns in the car.

LEWIS: Could have been anyone.

QUEENIE: What you mean?

LEWIS: He could have been framed by anyone.

QUEENIE: What do you mean?

LEWIS: Look. The man has enemies, the man knows too much.

QUEENIE: Like what?

LEWIS: Bad deeds. Corruption. Kickbacks. All his old buddies from the struggle.

QUEENIE: Who you talking about?

LEWIS: Everyone.

QUEENIE: Come on, Lewis, some of us are straight.

LEWIS: Some of us are rich.

QUEENIE: Damned cellphone! I've lost you!

LEWIS: I said – Life's a bitch!

QUEENIE: If I was sure he was innocent, I'd let him out tomorrow.

LEWIS: And the law?

QUEENIE: The law, my dear Lewis, is the law.

LEWIS: And?

QUEENIE: And right is right!

LEWIS: So, one day we find the cell door open ...

QUEENIE: I've lost you completely now!

LEWIS: Hello? Hello? Queenie?

QUEENIE: Yes? Yes?

LEWIS: I've got you back! So! Say one day we find the cell door open and Jimmy Longlegs has gone, and the Chief of Police cries, help, help, help, wolfie wolfie!

QUEENIE: Well. Well. Let's say he knew what was really going on.

LEWIS: What is really going on?

QUEENIE: Do I know what's going on?

LEWIS: Okay, so. Say he was framed, do we let him out or do we keep him in?

QUEENIE: What you mean?

LEWIS: I mean, do we let him out or do we keep him in?

QUEENIE: How do we decide?

LEWIS: We decide – what's best for us, what's best for business, what's best for the New South Africa.

QUEENIE: So. Do we let him out or do we keep him in?

LEWIS: I just don't know.

Scene 17
Bokkie's Study

LULU *is circling* BOKKIE, *who is sitting hunched with his back to us in his armchair.* LULU *throws various photographs, letters and post cards into his lap.*

LULU: This is Freda Gildenstein. You had a love affair with her from 1966 to 1969. You used to meet at a Fox Street hotel! While you were gefuffeling in the back streets of Jo'burg, mummy was pregnant with me! And this is Toodles Shakanovski. You met her at the Café Wien in Hillbrow before it became Hillbrow. She had a fake French accent! You only found out in 1972 that she came from Rosettenville! This is a post card from Cookie Lazarus, who writes here, 'I look forward passionately to being the second mother of your darling child!'. And this is a photograph of Blossom Nicolby-Smith. You used to spend dirty weekends with her at the Four Seasons Hotel in Durban!

BOKKIE: Rubbish!

LULU: And we won't mention the ongoing liaison with Dinky Cohen, your young secretary.

BOKKIE: How did you find all this out?

LULU: Mom put a private detective on you years ago.

40

BOKKIE: Oh my baby, I never knew you knew!

LULU: Well now you know!

BOKKIE: My little baby girl, my princess, I was trying to protect you!

LULU: I don't need protection!

BOKKIE: Your mother was cold beyond cold! An ice maiden! And a man is a man!

LULU: Pathetic!

BOKKIE: How can I make it up to you! What must I do? What do you want?

LULU: I want Jimmy 'Long Legs' Mangane free!

BOKKIE *rises, faces the audience, and sings.*

WHY IS A CITY ALWAYS A WOMAN?

Why is a city always a woman
And because she's a woman, almost always a whore
A man can possess her, he can love and caress her
But don't be fooled, when the chips are down, she's gone!

Berlin's a bitch, and Amsterdam is addled
I keep a little diary of the cities I have travelled
Venice thinks she's classy, Vienna, I find rather brassy
My little black book is full of the towns I have known!

Barcelona's a beauty, brings out the bull in me
Ancient Rome lies back, always ready for a grope
But when the spirit calls she prefers to service the Pope
Manhatten's a dry martini, she's fast paced and she's chic
I tried to bed her once, I just found the girl too slick

As for the rest of the cities – I find them all a bore
So I come back to Johannesburg
My little teenage whore
Every time I've gone away

And rampaged with another
I think this time its over
But my Jo' burg calls me back
My sweet little teenage lover

If the cities of the world are women
Then Jozi is my teenage whore
I love you Jozi Jozi
I'll never leave you any more

Jozi belonged to a pimp by the time she was ten
What can you expect she's a city made for men
She's known so many guys in her short and bold career
The gal is going crazy with gonorrhoea

The lights become shadowed and sinister. THE COMPANY *comes forward and whispers.*

If they steal – chop off the hand
If they lie – pull out the tongue
If they rape – cut, castrate
If in they put their foot – cut it off
If they smoke weed – cut out the lungs
If they drink – sew up their lips
If they walk the streets – sew up their little eyes
If they think bad thoughts – off with their heads!

Scene 18

A Melville Café

BONES *and* BOKKIE *sit on the pavement in the sun. Jackets off, ties pulled loose.*

BONES *and* BOKKIE: Crime! Crime! Crime!
BOKKIE: So, the other day I'm in Joubert Park.
BONES: Ja?

BOKKIE: I'm standing at a robot, kinda day dreaming – I'm looking at this kid sniffing glue. He's got a face like an angel ...

BONES: ...and he's sniffing glue.

BOKKIE: So anyway, a guy kinda dances into the road in front of me, his arms flapping and his face grinning, dances around to my left window, you know, and he just catches me off guard!

BONES: Off guard!

BOKKIE: Now I know all the scams, but he catches me off guard, and I'm screaming – get away from the window! Get away from the window! And the guys on the pavement next to the glue sniffer are laughing, and this guy on the pavement catches my face, you know?

BONES: The fear ...

BOKKIE: ... and he makes like a gorilla and shouts at me 'I'll kill you', 'I'll kill you', and he's growling, and we're both laughing, kinda embarrassed, because we both caught with our pants down, if you know what I mean?

BONES: With your pants down!

BOKKIE: ... and I grin and give him a thumbs up sign and then put my fukken foot down – the robot was green – you know what I mean?

BONES: So, what's crime, Boks?

BOKKIE: Things against the law.

BONES: Who's the law? What's the law, Who made the law? How sacred is the law? Who does this law protect? The innocent or the guilty? The criminal or the victim? Let me ask you? How old is crime?

BOKKIE: You asking me?

BONES: Crime is as young as your innocence, crime is as old as the missionaries of Satan. Crime is the first field of corn.

BOKKIE: Jo'burg is built on crime. From the first moment that they picked up the nugget of gold – crime!

BONES: The first factory?

BOKKIE: Crime!

BONES: The Johannesburg washer men, and the Johannesburg whores, the Johannesburg brick works?

BOKKIE: Crime!

BONES: The first tram running to Doornfontein?

BOKKIE: Nog crime!

BONES: Johannesburg is full of hard men, bitter men, men who just want to cut through the earth and the dust and make a buck!

BOKKIE: From all over the world they came to make this buck!

BONES: Don't think we didn't learn! Last year's illegal shebeen – this year's drinking tavern!

BOKKIE: A millionaire!

BONES: Last year's illegal shack – this year's housing project!

BOKKIE: Another millionaire!

BONES: Apartheid – the crime of the century, and now we just pick up the stick and run!

BOKKIE: I'm a gambling man myself. I like the tables. Can play all night. You know if I phone up any of these casinos at four in the morning – they open up for me!

BONES: Me, I like the horses. When the tail is like this – it means something, when it's like this, it means something. I like something to mean something.

BOKKIE: I gave up the horses when they started calling it the Siyafunda Sukuma Siye Phambili *(We learn We stand We go forward)* Plate!

BONES: What's your problem, umlungu *(white man)*? What's your problem!

BOKKIE: I don't dream in Zulu!

BONES: You and your dreams! Always filled with hot favourites! And where do they feature? Also Ran! You? Also an also ran! What horses do you back on? Horses with names like Headless Pilot – Barbed Wire – Hurry up Slowly! What kinda shmuck *(fool)* are you!

I'm talking poetic horses like Tiger Fish – Chamborah – Long Walk to Freedom – Zambian Princess – horses with names that sound like jewels, man! Ambitious Cassius! African Dream! Ethiopian Wonder! A horse that can think! A horse with hunger! A horse with mean hungry strides! A horse flying for the winning post! I like something to mean something!

BOKKIE: I'm a gambling man. Most of my chavers (*buddies*) have gone – all over the world. Me I'm staying. I'm staying right here in Johannesburg. I'm betting that everything's gonna be just fine!

BONES: Sure. Everything's gonna be just fine!

BOKKIE: So listen, let's not beat about the bush – my daughter tells me you know this Jimmy 'Long Legs' Mangane?

BONES: Sure.

BOKKIE: My daughter says you need a lot of money. Let's not fuck around, how much money do you need?

Scene 19

The Prison Cell

QUEENIE *bursts in on* JIMMY'S *cell and finds it empty. She howls out in rage.*

QUEENIE: Oh my God, an empty cell! He's gone! Jimmy 'Long Legs' Mangane is gone! [*She addresses the audience*] Bring me a pen! Bring me a pen! What kind of a police station is this with out a pen! Where are the chairs? Who's taken the tables?

Here I am, Chief of Police, and I can't even keep a prisoner locked up in a cell.

This job's impossible! My hands are tied behind my back. You need a photograph, there's no cameras. You need a statement, no pens! You need a finger print, no pads!

What is this place? You need a door open, it's locked! You need a door locked, it's open!

Well good for you, Jimmy! Show them what you're made of. You need a key, here's a key. You need a girl, then get a girl. If you need a road to the north, the road is good and long!

Am I the only person in this town who believes that criminals should be locked up?

THE COMPANY *sings:*

EVERYONE KNOWS WHERE HE IS
(IN THE SECRET SECRET SERVICE)

LULU: Everyone knows where he is
BONES: He's in her bed of course
LULU: Where else could he possibly be
    I've been planning this journey
    for him and for me
    But I can't make him stick to plan A, B or C
    Oh where could he possibly be?
Chorus:
    He's in the service
    The secret secret service
    He's in the service
    The secret secret service
LULU: Why do I love the wrong man?
    Can it be true what they say?
    He's a no good rotten sham
BIBI: … but a really classy lay!
BOKKIE: He's in her bed now,
    He's in the black whore's bed now
ALL: He's in her bed now
    He's in the black whore's bed now
LULU: He's impossible to hold
    He's impossible to know
    Tries to make me love him more
BIBI: …but he comes back to his whore!
JIMMY: A man of vision,
    He is a man of vision
ALL: A man of vision,
    He is a man of vision
LULU: Why does he drive me so wild?
    Why does she keep us apart?
    Why does he make me a child?
BIBI: He wants to cut up your heart!

BONES: He likes the trigger
  He likes to pull the trigger
ALL: He likes the trigger
  He likes to pull the trigger
LULU: Why can't I keep him aflame?
  Why does her smell light his fire?
  When I give him all I've got
BIBI: Still it's me that he desires!
ALL: Can the secret service keep a secret?
  Everywhere corruption – we don't see it
(LULU: And I love the wrong man)
  The serpent is arising and we feed it
(LULU: And I love the wrong man)
  Before they close the papers we can read it
(LULU: And I love the wrong man)

Repeat

ALL: And she loves the wrong man!

Scene 20
The Doorway

BONES *stands and addresses the audience.*

BONES: I've lived a long life, I've seen too many terrible things. In the prisons, in the apartheid prisons, the gangs fill the guts of the traitor with hard porridge, stiff porridge. Then the moment comes. They execute the traitor by delivery of blows to the stomach! No marks … another mysterious death! This is not the way for a man to die! We want a clean death! An honourable death!

  I am very tired. I have seen too many terrible things. I feel close to the end. It is time for me to die. I want to die. I hope when I die, I will see just one small glimpse of the face of my maker. Then it will be darkness forever.

Scene 21

A Melville Café

JIMMY *enters the café and rather surreptitiously finds a seat.*
Moments later, LULU *enters and hurriedly joins him.*

LULU: Thank God you made it! Are you all right? Did you have any
   problems? You look all puffy.

JIMMY: I'm fine. I'm here.

LULU: I'm all organised. God, I missed you.

[*The two lovers kiss passionately.*]

> The passport's here. I've filled the Merc with petrol. Oh my
> darling, just be careful with the car – you know my dad. The
> Merc's like his wife. Oh my darling, are you gonna be all right?

JIMMY: Sure! Sure!

LULU: The map book's in the cubby hole. The Merc takes unleaded.
   I parked the car at C level at Sandton City. Oh, you look so tense,
   my darling, it's all over now. By the way, your name in the passport
   is Zwelakhe Levine.

JIMMY: Zwelakhe Levine!

LULU: Well, we're going to be together, so it makes sense. [*She
   kisses him.*] Now, let's see, you haven't forgotten the plan?

> I've got the car keys. You collect the car. Take the airport road.
> Just don't stop for anyone. Your papers are all in order. There
> won't be any problem at the border. You know the routine. The
> same border crossing you always used in the old days. You can
> do this in your sleep. I've packed a suitcase with some mineral
> water. I can't remember what the water's like there. Once you've
> crossed the border, look for the signs for the cuddle puddle. Then
> the turn off to the hot springs. Apparently it's lovely. My parents
> had their honeymoon there. You'll be very comfortable. Just keep
> a low profile. You must only order room service. You know how
> famous you are.

JIMMY: I'll be okay.

LULU: You can never be too careful.

JIMMY: Sure.

LULU: Rest, recover, I'll join you there in two days time. We can spend an easy time together, reconnecting, not having to worry about anything. We'll clear your name, plan your political comeback. I'll look after you.

[*She kisses him again.*]

We can get married in your own good time, no pressure. Jimmy! I can't wait. You and I together, using our energies, fighting for what's right! We'll clear your name, you'll come back the people's hero you've always been.

JIMMY: Lulu, I knew I could rely on you. Through thick and thin. Did you bring any cash?

LULU: Of course.

LULU *hands over a bundle.* JIMMY *hides it.*

LULU: Oh my darling, free at last! Kiss me!

Scene 22

The Office of the Chief of Police

At the desk LEWIS is leaning over QUEENIE as he gives her the news.

LEWIS: Queenie Dlamini, I'm sorry to tell you,
    Your job is on the line, you broke all the rules
    You planned Jimmy 'Long Legs''s escape from jail,
    You just can't do all that stuff, you fool!

QUEENIE: What are you telling me, what do you mean?
    I had nothing to do with him running free.
    I was fighting dark and dastardly crimes,
    Don't you try pinning his escape on me!

LEWIS: The New South Africa has to save face,
    The action you took was totally against the law.
    Too bad. The constitution sits in place,
    Chief of Police takes the rap. You know the score.

49

QUEENIE: The legal route! Have you gone crazy?

Play by the rules, we'll be dead, we'll be hounded!

LEWIS: You did something real silly!

Going for corruption wherever you found it.

QUEENIE: What you mean, don't give me that shit!

I tried to get their dirty fingers out the purse!

LEWIS: You tried to put a Senior Man behind bars,

QUEENIE: Stealing the country blind! He was a curse!

LEWIS: So what if he had his hand in the till,

He was loyal to the President.

QUEENIE: This job's impossible, the country's full of crime,

Every gangster's rights mean so much more than mine.

Criminals do what they like – you expect me to toe the line!

LEWIS: Use the police force properly!

QUEENIE: The police! My police don't give a damn!

LEWIS: Justice must be done and seen!

QUEENIE: It seems that being crooked is the only plan.

LEWIS: Yes, well, being crooked gets you further than being clean!

QUEENIE: Justice must be done and seen!

LEWIS: Don't worry, you're getting a golden handshake – nine hundred thousand Rand!

QUEENIE: I think I'll buy a town house in Cape Town, next to yours! Right on the strand!

QUEENIE *breaks out into a wildly celebratory religious song.*

THE COMPANY *changes the set.*

Scene 23

A Cheap Bruma Lake Hotel Room

JIMMY *and* BIBI *are making love under the sheets.* BONES *stands quietly at the door.*

JIMMY: Oh Bibi, oh Bibi, give it to me baby! Yoo! Don't move, don't move, ooh, baby, move, move, move! No stay still, you got it, baby –

Mtanyam …

Ooh, ooh, you look like your mother when she was pregnant with me!

Oh my baby, I love you! I'm gonna take you to my home, I'm gonna let you meet my mother and father! Oh baby don't move, don't move, I love you!

BIBI: Aaaah aaah aaah aaahmandla! Jimmy 'Long Legs'!

As JIMMY and BIBI *reach their climax*, BONES *speaks*. JIMMY, *startled, snatches for the sheet and tries to hide his body*. BIBI *grabs the duvet. Enter* QUEENIE, LULU *and* BOKKIE.

BONES: 'Long Legs' se gat!

JIMMY: Ah, Papa Bones!

BONES: Papa Bones, my arse!

JIMMY: Ah, Bra Bones, let me explain!

BONES: Explain! Explain! I give you the key, the right key! What do you do? You open the bloody wrong door!

JIMMY: Bones, please …

BONES: My lewe is op die lyn (*My life is on the line*), and what you doing!!! You have given up your chance, because you can only smell women! U phatesitswe ka mpapa! (*You are bewitched by vaginas!*)

JIMMY: Ah Bones …

BONES: Do you think I click my fingers and prison doors all over Jo'burg spring open?! Is that what you think! Masipa antatwa man! (*Shit, man!*) I spent money! I pulled strings! I begged favours! So that you could dip your one-eyed wonder in that used up piece of street tart!

My dignity is rotting in daai squeeza (*that girlfriend*) you swimming in!

You smell a woman and you lose your mind! You're meant to be over the border! What happened to the plan?

LULU: Jimmy you fool, you could have had me. So long my darling, my sweetheart, my poet! I never want to see you again!

BOKKIE: You tell her my sweetie – Buafela! (*Tell her!*)

BONES: Let me tell you my boy – you gonna go to jail, and there, the only piece of arse you ever gonna get near is gonna have a cock attached to the front!

QUEENIE, *triumphant, climbs on the bed.*

QUEENIE: Well, well! A lovely family reunion! So, my dear Jimmy, as we all could have predicted, sex got you in the end! My dear boy, C-Max waits for you! It's back to prison with you, this time for ever!

JIMMY [*looking up at her and singing*]: Don't hang me by the neck, you can't do that any more.

ALL: All these brutal acts, They are now against the law!

THE COMPANY *sings*:

SONG OF THE CONSTITUTION

 Three cheers for the Constitutional Court
 Hooray, hooray, hooray
 A glowing diamond high up there on the skyline
 Three cheers for the Constitutional Court
 Hooray, Hooray, Hooray
 There's so much more to gain when you're walking the thin line

JIMMY: We can do anything that we want

ALL: And can they string us up by the neck – No!

LULU: We can say and write what we like

ALL: And can they string us up by the neck – No!

BOKKIE: Free to worship as we please

ALL: And can they string us up by the neck – No!

BIBI: We can catch any slimy disease

ALL: And can they string us up by the neck – No!

Chorus:

 Mealies First
 You've got to give us something we can savour
 Feed us first, we'll talk about the moral issues later!
 Three cheers for the Constitutional Court (etc)

QUEENIE: Watch out for women, we've got rights

ALL: And can they string us up by the neck – No!

LULU: We can taste all kinds of delights
ALL: And can they string us up by the neck – No!
LEWIS: Talk of language, anything goes
ALL: And can they string us up by the neck   No!
JIMMY: Zulu, Sotho, Pedi [BONES *joins in*] and prose
ALL: *And can they string us up by the neck – No!*
Chorus:
Mealies first …

Scene 24

The Public Square

The CHIEF OF POLICE *ushers* JIMMY 'LONG LEGS' MANGANE *to centre stage. Once again, he is heavily chained in leg irons and handcuffs. In spite of this, he is still smiling charmingly.*

QUEENIE: Jimmy 'Long Legs' Mangane, you have a life sentence! Before you are taken to maximum security to rot, sealed up in a cell until you die, do you have anything to say? This is your last chance!
JIMMY *takes centre stage*
JIMMY: Should I stand up here, begging for forgiveness?
Yes, I would, if I understood the crime.
I stare at the glazed looks on your faces
It's clear to me you don't give one damn
And so I have to say it once again
You think that crime will stop if you lock me in
But we live in hell, others continue to sin
Let us wash our sins away, we clearly need the rain

And so I stand here and I surprise myself
I ask forgiveness, in hope the good Lord hears
But all our thoughts and plans and clever deeds
Bite the dust, and leave us ash and tears

And so I face my fate!
QUEENIE: Take him to jail to rot!

There is a triumphant musical call from THE COMPANY.
LEWIS *enters carrying a long fax.*
LEWIS: Wait! Wait! Wait! Silence!

I bring news, important news, from the President's office. [*He unrolls the document.*] Hear this, hear this, all South Africans! On the occasion of the inauguration of the third President of the Democratic Republic of South Africa – given that none of us knows what's right and wrong, given that we put our brutal past behind us, given that only a few pass through the narrow gates of heaven, and given that reconciliation has so perfectly been achieved – there will be, with immediate effect, for all gangsters, politicians, criminals and businessmen, a general amnesty!

THE COMPANY *rises in a slow motion, silent, cheer*
LEWIS: The new President of this great democracy declares a general amnesty for all! Jimmy 'Long Legs' Mangane – you are free!
There is a second triumphant musical call from THE COMPANY.
JIMMY *praises the gods.*
THE COMPANY [*turns to the audience and sings*]:

RESTORE ALL TO ORDER (IN PERFECT HARMONY)

There is a reprieve, a general amnesty
For who is to say who is right and who is wrong
The rich are still rich, the poor desperately poor
Ag man, its true! Only the chosen ones belong

Dog eat dog, shark eat shark
In an African Babylon
Dog eat dog, shark eat shark
Who knows what's going on?

What we propose.
Is forgive everyone

Light of the millennium calls us
There's bound to be peace in the age to come
Let's grit our teeth and bear the journey
All will be well in a hundred years' time

Yes it will

And all will be well in a hundred years' time!

Blackout.

Printed and bound by CPI Group (UK) Ltd, Croydon, CR0 4YY

14/04/2025

14656907-0001